P9-CSG-525

Louis Armstrong and the Jazz Age

CORNERSTONES OF FREEDOM™

SECOND SERIES

Dan Elish

Children's Press®
A Division of Scholastic Inc.
New York • Toronto • London • Auckland • Sydney
Mexico City • New Delhi • Hong Kong
Danbury, Connecticut

26.00

Photographs © 2005: akg-images: 31 (IMS), 39; AP/Wide World Photos: cover top, 26, 34; Brown Brothers: 11; Greg Copeland: 10; Corbis Images: 3, 19 bottom, 21, 29, 35, 36, 44 center, 45 bottom (Bettmann), 19 top (Underwood & Underwood), 5 (Ted Williams), 17, 32; Corbis Sygma/Pierre Fournier: 40; Frank Driggs Collection: 23, 25, 44 top, 45 top left; Getty Images/Frank Driggs Collection: cover bottom; Hogan Jazz Archive/Tulane University: 12; Hulton|Archive/Getty Images: 8, 24, 45 top right (Frank Driggs Collection), 9 (Evans), 33 (Weegee (Arthur Fellig)/International Centre for Photography), 27; Louis Armstrong House & Archives at Queens College: 13, 14, 15; North Wind Picture Archives: 6; PictureQuest/Spencer Grant: 4, 44 bottom; Stock Montage, Inc.: 22; Superstock, Inc.: 38 (Joseph Barnell), 7 (Christie's Images), 30 (Culver Pictures, Inc.), 41 right; The Art Archive/Picture Desk/National Archives, Washington, DC: 20; The Image Works/Topham: 18, 41 left.

Library of Congress Cataloging-in-Publication Data
Elish, Dan.
  Louis Armstrong and the jazz age / Dan Elish.—1st ed.
    p. cm. — (Cornerstones of freedom. Second series)
  ISBN 0-516-23629-6
  1. Armstrong, Louis, 1901–1971—Juvenile literature. 2. Jazz musicians—United States—Biography—Juvenile literature. 3. Jazz—History and criticism—Juvenile literature. I. Title. II. Series: Cornerstones of freedom. Second series.
ML3930.A75E54 2005
781.65'3—dc22

                                        2004010663

Copyright © 2005 Scholastic Inc.
All rights reserved. Published simultaneously in Canada.
Printed in the United States of America.

CHILDREN'S PRESS, and CORNERSTONES OF FREEDOM™, and associated logos are trademarks and or registered trademarks of Scholastic Library Publishing. SCHOLASTIC and associated logos are trademarks and or registered trademarks of Scholastic Inc.

1 2 3 4 5 6 7 8 9 10 R 14 13 12 11 10 09 08 07 06 05

IN THE SUMMER OF 1922, A YOUNG man named Louis Armstrong boarded a train headed for Chicago. He carried a small suitcase, a fish sandwich prepared by his mother, and a **cornet**. Though he was only twenty-one, Louis was already known as one of the best musicians in New Orleans. His specialty was a new kind of music called jazz.

Growing up, Louis bought a used cornet and taught himself how to play. A cornet is similar to a trumpet.

THE CORNET

The cornet is a brass musical instrument that looks like a shortened trumpet. Cornets and trumpets have the same range, but the cornet has a softer tone. Louis Armstrong started his career playing the cornet, but most of his recordings are on the trumpet.

Now Louis had been invited to join a band headed by Joe Oliver. Oliver was one of the best cornet players in the country. When Louis finally arrived in Chicago it was close to midnight. "I saw a million people," he said later, "but not Mister Joe. . . . I was just fixing to take the next train back home."

Luckily young Louis gathered his wits and flagged a cab. He rode to Lincoln Gardens, the most popular jazz club in the black section of Chicago. Standing outside, Louis could hear Oliver's group playing. He thought, "I wonder if I'm good enough to play in that band?"

* * * *

As it turned out, Louis had nothing to worry about. During the next decade, a period often called the Jazz Age, jazz would become America's most important **native** art form. During this time, Louis Armstrong played a vital role in the development of jazz.

BEGINNINGS IN NEW ORLEANS

Jazz is a musical style based on **improvisation**, or the art of making something up on the spot. Today many people have experienced the thrill of hearing a saxophone player or a trumpet player step in front of a band and improvise part of a song. But this form of free musical expression didn't

Today, jazz is celebrated in many parts of the world. This saxophone player is performing at a jazz festival in Newport, Rhode Island.

exist one hundred years ago. Most musicians were trained to follow written notes. Over time, several musical styles came together to form what we now call jazz. And the place it all began was New Orleans, Louisiana.

New Orleans was founded by the French in 1718. From the beginning, the city attracted many types of people who played many types of music. Before the Civil War, slaves in New Orleans were allowed to perform African songs and dances in a place called Congo Square. Slaves from the West Indies sang with the rhythms of the Caribbean. Slaves from the South sang work songs and spirituals. As these musical styles blended together, slaves began to improvise words and tunes. Meanwhile, those who played instruments began to improvise around written dance music.

This illustration shows one artist's view of the city of New Orleans in 1718.

This Albert Bloch painting shows partygoers enjoying the rhythmic beat of ragtime music, which was popular in the early 1900s.

Toward the turn of the twentieth century, a new music called ragtime swept across the country. It was lively music with a jumpy, rhythmic beat. At the same time, a large number of African Americans from Mississippi came to New Orleans. They sang about their feelings in a simple form called the blues. Creoles, who were part French, added their classical musical training to the mix. The city was also home to a large number of **brass bands**. These bands played everything from spiritual music to ragtime.

New Orleans was special in another way too. At the time, blacks were treated horribly by whites throughout the South. But in New Orleans black and white musicians often played music together. As one black musician remembered, "It didn't really matter what color you were." Musicians of different races traded ideas, and jazz was born.

BUDDY BOLDEN

The most famous early jazz cornet player was Buddy Bolden. Born in 1877, "King" Bolden played louder and bolder than anyone who had come before. He was an inspiration to young Louis Armstrong. Louis once said, "People thought he was plumb crazy the way he tossed that horn."

Louis grew up in New Orleans with his mother, Mayann (center), and his sister, Beatrice (right).

GROWING UP IN STORYVILLE

Louis liked to say that he was born on July 4, 1900. Most evidence, however, suggests that August 4, 1901, was his actual birthday. Whatever the date, Louis was born into difficult circumstances. His father, William, moved out of the house shortly after Louis was born. That left Louis and his sister, Beatrice, in the care of their mother, Mary Ann (also known as Mayann). She was just a teenager when Louis was born.

Louis's family lived in a poor section of New Orleans called "Black" Storyville. There, families lived in small one-story homes. There was no indoor plumbing. In order to bathe, people had to boil water and pour it into a small tub. Mary Ann worked on and off as a maid. As a boy, Louis got used to spending time with his grandmother. He also got used to having nothing.

At about age seven, Louis got a job working for a Russian Jewish family. The Karnofskys hired Louis to blow a

Louis was born in this house, at 723 Jane Place, New Orleans. This photograph was taken around 1960.

horn to attract attention to their junk wagon, which they rolled through the streets selling coal. The family took a liking to young Louis. They always made sure that he got a good meal before he went home. To his dying day, Louis remembered their kindness by wearing a Star of David, a symbol of **Judaism**, around his neck.

9

Street performers were common in New Orleans. They brought energy and life to a city filled with music.

Between jobs, Louis took in the sights and sounds of the city. When he was a boy, New Orleans had a world-class opera company, several fine orchestras, and hundreds of marching bands. Louis soon added his own talents to the mix. He formed a vocal quartet—a singing group with four members—with

10

* * * *

friends. He and his group sang on street corners for pennies. Louis used the money to help support his family.

Still, Louis's musical training might have ended there. As he said later, "I remember running around with a lot of bad boys that did a lot of crazy things." The craziest thing happened one New Year's Eve. In Storyville people celebrated the new year by setting off fireworks and shooting guns. That night Louis performed with his quartet on the city streets.

At midnight Louis pulled a gun that belonged to his step-father out of his coat. It is unclear whether the gun was

FIRST JAZZ RECORD

In 1917, a group of white musicians called the Original Dixieland Jazz Band became the first band to record jazz. Thousands of copies of their recordings were sold, and Americans suddenly went crazy for jazz. The group's leader, Nick LaRocca, insisted that jazz was the creation of whites. But it is clear that the band's music was heavily influenced by the many black musicians they had met and heard in New Orleans.

The Original Dixieland Jazz Band was from New Orleans, but had to travel to New York to make records. Most jazz bands got famous through record companies that were based in New York or Chicago.

loaded with blanks or with real bullets. Louis fired once over his head, making what he called "a whole gang of sound." The next thing he knew two white arms were wrapped around his chest. It was a policeman. Louis was under arrest!

THE WAIF'S HOME

Louis spent the next year and a half at the Colored Waif's Home. It was a place known for reforming **wayward** children. The rules were strict. Boys were expected to rise at dawn, march in groups, do chores, and study.

There was also time for fun. From the day he arrived, young Louis was desperate to join the home's brass band. The leader was a man named Peter Davis. Davis was suspicious of boys who came from Louis's tough neighborhood. But a few

After his arrest, Louis was sent to the Waif's Home. He lived there off and on throughout his teenage years.

This photograph shows Louis (back row, center) in the Waif's Home Band around 1913.

months later Davis approached Louis and asked, "How would you like to play in the band?"

Though Louis first played the tambourine, Davis quickly recognized his remarkable ability. Within weeks Louis was the school bugler. He soon earned the nicknames "Gatemouth" and "Satchelmouth" due to the large size of his mouth. Later in his career, "Satchelmouth" would be shortened to "Satchmo." He was also called "Pops."

A NATURAL-BORN ENTERTAINER

"I remember Louis used to walk funny, with his feet pointing out, and at the first note of music he'd break into comedy dances. I'd play the horn and he'd dance, then when I'd put my horn down he'd pick it up and start playing it."

—Peter Davis, Armstrong's first bandleader

After a few months, the Waif band played a concert in Louis's old neighborhood. Louis's family and friends found it hard to believe that he had gotten so good so fast. Though they were poor, the people of Storyville dropped enough coins in the boys' hats to pay for new instruments and uniforms for the entire band.

Louis was well liked by the other children. He enjoyed his time at the home so much that he was almost disappointed on the day of his release, in June 1914. He left the Waif's Home with an even stronger passion for making music.

LOUIS PLAYS NEW ORLEANS

This photograph shows Louis (left) with "King" Oliver around 1923.

Louis Armstrong spent his teenage years playing the trumpet at parades, dance halls, and bars. He amazed older musicians with the power and creativity of his playing.

He also paid close attention to the music around him. Louis's favorite band was led by Joe Oliver. Oliver's band played at some of the city's toughest clubs. It was said that Oliver blew so hard when he played that he would blow a cornet out of tune every few months.

"King" Oliver took a liking to Louis and gave him cornet lessons. When people around town saw that Oliver had taken Louis under his

As a teenager, Louis
played his cornet around
New Orleans.

wing, they began to ask Louis to play at some of the better clubs.

Soon Joe Oliver left town to play in Chicago. In New Orleans, Louis was invited to join one of the best bands in town. The leader was a trombone player named Kid Ory. Ory said, "There were many good . . . trumpet players in town, but none of them had young Louis's possibilities. I told him that if he got himself a pair of long **trousers** I'd give him a job."

Louis loved playing in Kid Ory's band. He then spent summers of his late teenage years playing aboard steamships that chugged between New Orleans and St. Paul, Minnesota. Louis's **technique** improved. As he grew, his chest filled out, and his lips and jaw got stronger. He could play difficult high notes more easily.

By the time he was twenty-one Louis was one of the best-known players in New Orleans. Then came a note from Joe Oliver: Louis was invited to play in Chicago. "I always knew," Louis said later, "that if I was going to get a little break in this game, it was gonna be through Joe, nobody else."

AMERICA AFTER WORLD WAR I

At the dawn of the 1920s, the world Louis Armstrong had grown up in was rapidly changing. In 1917, America sent troops to Europe to fight in World War I. In 1919, Congress passed the Eighteenth Amendment to the United States Constitution, outlawing the sale of alcohol. On January 16, 1920, the Volstead Act went into effect. This

After the war, soldiers wave goodbye to Camp Dix, which served as a training ground for U.S. soldiers.

act strengthened the amendment, making it illegal to sell or transport any **beverage** containing more than one-half of one percent of alcohol. This period in American history is known as Prohibition.

Some people supported these new laws. They thought that **prohibiting** the use of alcohol would make people act more responsibly. Instead it had the opposite effect. Young

F. SCOTT FITZGERALD

F. Scott Fitzgerald was a well-known American writer. Born in 1896, Fitzgerald wrote many stories that captured the mood of the Jazz Age. He described the period as "living at top speed in the gayest world we could find." Fitzgerald's *The Great Gatsby* is considered one of America's greatest novels.

F. Scott Fitzgerald's novels and short stories tell about life during the Jazz Age.

Americans were ready to put the horrors of war behind them and celebrate the fun side of life. Speakeasies, or secret bars where people could drink, sprung up overnight.

At the same time, a dance craze swept through the nation. Older Americans were shocked as young people stayed up all night learning strange dances such as the Turkey Trot and the Charleston. The relaxed, carefree spirit of the time had the most obvious effect on women, many of whom began to smoke and wear short dresses. Some of the more modern women, called flappers, thought nothing of having a drink in a speakeasy. These "wild" times were also known as the Roaring Twenties.

It was the beginning of a newer, more modern age. The horse-and-buggy had been replaced by the automobile. People could even travel to other cities by plane. As the stock market soared, many Americans had extra money to spend. Jazz music was the perfect sound for this new, daring, and fast-paced world.

The short skirts, bobbed hair, and kicking heels of these young women were typical of flappers in 1920s Chicago.

This photograph captures a young couple dancing the Charleston in 1926.

19

By the early 1920s, Chicago had moved ahead of New Orleans as the jazz capital of the country. This is a view of Chicago's State Street shopping district.

"LITTLE" LOUIS HITS CHICAGO

Once Louis arrived in Chicago, Joe Oliver arranged for his room and board. He lived in a South Side rooming house with his own private bathroom. Louis was amazed. He had never even heard of a bathtub with running water.

In those days, most jazz bands used only one trumpet. But when Oliver asked Louis to join him he was interested

African Americans move their belongings in a South Side neighborhood in 1919.

in trying something new. For the next two years, the two men perfected their own style. Usually Oliver would take the lead while Louis played a melody line to go with it. Other times, they would trade solos, playing off each other while the band **accompanied** them.

As always, Louis's playing attracted attention. Soon, word of Oliver and Louis's new and exciting sound was sweeping across the jazz world. Many well-known white musicians came to Lincoln Gardens to see the young trumpet player. Songwriter Hoagy Carmichael remembered thinking, "Why isn't everyone in the world here to hear this?"

On April 25, 1923, Oliver's band traveled to Richmond, Indiana, to make a record. At that time, making a record meant that musicians had to first play into a giant horn. The horn then transferred, or moved, the sound to a wax disc, creating a record. It is said that Louis's playing was so forceful

King Oliver's Creole Jazz Band took Chicago by storm. Armstrong is shown kneeling in front with a slide trumpet, and King Oliver is playing the cornet behind him.

"KING" OLIVER

Not all the great musicians of the Jazz Age achieved the fame and fortune that Louis Armstrong did. By 1928, Joe Oliver had trouble getting enough jobs to keep his band working. Then America was hit by a great depression that hurt record sales. By the mid-1930s, "King" Oliver was running a fruit stand in Savannah, Georgia, and working as a janitor in a pool hall. He died in 1938.

he had to stand behind the other musicians so that his cornet wouldn't be the loudest instrument on the recording.

The main cornet sound belonged to Oliver, but Louis was allowed to play solo on a song called "Chimes Blues." The difference between Louis's playing and Oliver's was striking. While Oliver used a **mute** to soften the sound of his cornet, Louis let loose with a brasher tone. His style was different from anything that anyone had heard before.

Soon after his arrival in Chicago, Louis was introduced to Lillian (Lil) Hardin. She was a young piano player in Oliver's band. After studying music at Fisk University, Lil headed for Chicago. She was quickly recognized as a leading jazz player.

Louis and Lillian Hardin posed for this picture taken in Hollywood in 1930.

* * * *

At first sight, Lil wasn't impressed with Louis. "Everything he had on was too small for him," she said. She thought it was ridiculous that someone who weighed 226 pounds (102.5 kilograms) should be called "Little" Louis. It didn't take long, though, for Lil to be charmed by Louis's good nature and brilliant playing. Louis had married a woman in New Orleans when he was very young, but Lil helped him arrange a divorce. The couple then married on February 5, 1924.

From the beginning, Lil was determined to get Louis out from under Joe Oliver's shadow. She pushed for Louis to strike out on his own. She also insisted that he lose weight and buy new clothes.

Louis had no plans to leave the man who had done so much for him. But when other band members quit after arguing about their pay, Louis finally decided to leave. With no job, Louis waited for his next big break.

NEW YORK CITY

In the early 1920s a young black man named Fletcher Henderson had come to New York City. At first he'd hoped to pursue a career in chemistry. Over time he put down his books and performed on the piano. He soon became head of the Black Swan Troubadours, one of the leading black dance bands in the city.

Henderson's band was made up of well-trained musicians who played popular dance tunes. They had a standing gig,

Fletcher Henderson was the leader of a dance band in New York. His band became particularly well known after Louis Armstrong joined in 1924.

PAUL WHITEMAN

Not all jazz musicians were black. In fact, the man most responsible for bringing this new music to the majority of Americans was a white **conductor** named Paul Whiteman. Whiteman was the first musician to play jazz with a full orchestra.

In February 1924, Whiteman organized a jazz concert in New York City. One performer was a young composer named George Gershwin. His piece "Rhapsody in Blue" became the most famous jazz orchestral composition of its time. Whiteman became known as "the king of jazz" due to his ability to promote this new music.

Paul Whiteman was one of America's best-known bandleaders. He is shown here conducting his orchestra in 1935.

or job, at the Roseland Ballroom. But as well as the Black Swans played, they didn't have a natural improviser like Louis. Louis could add zip to any dance number with a heart-pounding solo. On a trip to New Orleans in 1922, Henderson had heard Louis play. "I never forgot that kid," he said later. "Louis was even better than Oliver. . . . I had to try to get him for my band."

In 1924, Louis moved to New York to play in Fletcher Henderson's band. But when Louis arrived at his first rehearsal, his new bandmates weren't impressed. According to one player, Louis was "big and fat and wore high-top shoes with hooks in them and long underwear down to his socks." Another thought, "That can't be Louis Armstrong."

Louis was a star soloist. However, he was not nearly as good at sight reading, or reading notes that were written down. As a result, Henderson gave him less music to play

Louis's enthusiasm and spontaneity made him a favorite with audiences.

than the other trumpet players. Still, it didn't take long for Louis to make his mark. Using no written music, Louis simply waited for the solo breaks. Then he would play his head off.

Soon the band composer was writing pieces to show off Louis's incredible sense of rhythm. Though no one named it at the time, Louis was inventing a rhythmic sound called swing. He called it a way of "cutting loose and taking the music with you." He went on: "It takes a swing player, and a real good one, to be able to leave that [written] score and to know, or 'feel,' just when to leave it and when to get back on it."

Louis's influence on the New York jazz world was enormous. Every jazz band in town suddenly began trying to "swing." Louis became the idol, or hero, of many musicians. Trumpet player Rex Stewart said, "I tried to walk like him, talk like him, eat like him, sleep like him. I even bought a pair of big policeman shoes like he used to wear and stood outside his apartment waiting for him to come out so I could look at him." Just as he had with Chicago, Louis took New York by storm.

HARLEM

Years later Louis described his move to New York this way: "I could blow all right, but . . . in that big town I was just a little small-town boy and nobody much on Broadway had ever heard of me. But Harlem saved my life."

Harlem is a neighborhood in upper Manhattan in New York City. In the Jazz Age it was home to many great black artists of the era. Louis quickly found an apartment in

In the 1920s, Harlem was one of the cultural centers of New York. Here, entertainers gather at a club in Harlem in 1929.

Harlem. He drank up the energy that went with being part of a vibrant and artistic black community. After playing with Fletcher Henderson at Roseland, Louis would head uptown for late-night practice sessions.

During the Jazz Age, many white Americans became fascinated by black culture. By the mid-1920s, whites were

The Cotton Club opened on 142nd St. and Lenox Ave. in Manhattan in 1922. The musicians, dancers, and waiters were all African American, but the audience was mostly white.

traveling uptown to Harlem on weekends to sample the food, admire the energy, and hear the music. Clubs such as the Savoy and the Cotton Club featured some of the best entertainment of the decade.

* * * *

One of the most notable musicians was Duke Ellington. Raised in Washington, D.C., Ellington moved to New York in 1923. He then took over a band that became popular in Times Square. When Ellington first saw Louis at Roseland, he said that he had finally heard "that missing something." After that, Ellington changed his band to add more rhythmic punch or "swing."

From 1927 until 1932 Ellington's band played at the Cotton Club. It was there that Ellington developed his own

Duke Ellington was a popular pianist, arranger, composer, and bandleader during the Jazz Age.

A VIEW OF HARLEM

"You get the full essence of

Harlem in an air shaft. You

hear fights, you smell

dinner. . . . You hear intimate

gossip floating down. You hear

the radio. . . . You see your

neighbor's laundry. You hear

the janitor's dogs. . . . You smell

coffee. . . . You hear people

praying, fighting, snoring."

—Duke Ellington, 1940

This portrait of the Hot Five
was taken in the 1930s.
Its members were (from left
to right) Johnny St. Cyr,
Edward "Kid" Ory, Louis
Armstrong, Johnny Dodds,
and Lillian Armstrong.

jazz style. When his band was broadcast by radio into homes across the country, Ellington became known as one of jazz's leading composers.

THE HOT FIVE

Although Louis had some success in New York, he would soon move back to Chicago. His wife, Lil, had stayed there and she eventually led a band of her own. When her band got a job at a well-known Chicago dance club, the Dreamland Cafe, she asked Louis to come back.

Soon after his return to Chicago, Louis was invited to record songs at Okeh Records. Louis brought along four players, including his wife, Lil, on the piano and his old bandleader Kid Ory on trombone. They called themselves the Hot Five.

Louis is shown here singing with Velma Middleton around 1940.

During the next three years, Louis recorded sixty-five songs with this group and with another called the Hot Seven. Most experts consider these recordings the greatest in jazz history.

The Hot Five recordings also introduced Louis's singing to the world. Today many people know Louis mainly as a singer. Early in his career, however, most musicians didn't take his singing seriously. In New York, Louis begged Fletcher Henderson to let him sing. But Henderson always said no. Then, one night Louis sang in front of a crowd and brought down the house. Henderson finally changed his mind.

What really set Louis's singing apart was his ability to scat. Scatting is singing a song using a jumble of syllables and sounds instead of actual lyrics, or words. The story goes

JAZZ SLANG

Throughout the years jazz musicians have become known for their slang. Louis Armstrong often used the word "cat" to refer to a person. The term later became popular. In the Jazz Age, Americans coined lots of slang terms, including

- *dewdropper*—someone who slept all day and didn't have a job
- *moonshine*—homemade whiskey
- *scratch*—money
- *whoopee*—wild fun

33

BIX BEIDERBECKE

One of the best early jazz musicians was a white cornet player named Leon "Bix" Beiderbecke. However, because Bix was white he suffered a kind of reverse **discrimination**. As a white man he was not allowed to play in public with blacks, who were often the best musicians of this era. Bix became an alcoholic and died at age twenty-eight in 1931. "Lots of cats try to play like Bix," Louis said once. "Ain't none of them play like him yet."

Leon "Bix" Beiderbecke was born in Davenport, Iowa, in 1903. Against his parents' wishes, he later moved to Chicago to play jazz.

★ ★ ★ ★

that Louis introduced "scat" to the public by accident. While recording a song called "Heebie Jeebies," Louis accidentally dropped the lyric sheet. Instead of stopping, he began to scat for the first time on a recording. The record was a smash. In black neighborhoods, one musician said, "you would hear cats greeting each other with Louis's riffs. [His] scatting almost drove the English language out of the Windy City for good."

HOT CHOCOLATES

Although he was shy, Louis loved the feeling of being center stage. After the success of the Hot Five and Hot Seven recordings, he was in great demand in Chicago. As he put it, "There was more work than a cat could shake a stick at."

But the speakeasies where jazz musicians played were controlled by criminals. In 1928, Chicago finally started to crack down on the illegal sale of alcohol. Police officers closed down speakeasies. With many jazz clubs in Chicago shut, Louis traveled to New York and played a successful concert at the Savoy Theater in Harlem. It wasn't long before Louis wanted to try his luck on Broadway.

In 1929, Louis's manager, Tommy Rockwell, found him the break he needed. Rockwell got

Speakeasies were closed down after federal agents began to seize large amounts of illegal alcohol.

Enthusiastic fans surround Louis at Brooklyn College.

Louis a job in the pit, or orchestra, of a new Broadway show called *Great Day*. On the drive back to New York Louis began to realize just how popular he had become. In town after town, he heard his records being played on the radio and in homes. Strangers treated Louis and his band like kings. Fans refused to let them pay for meals and hotel rooms.

Unfortunately when Louis and his band reached New York, the white conductor of *Great Day* began to fire the black musicians in the orchestra. Soon after the show flopped. Louis still had his chance to appear on Broadway, though. In June he played the trumpet in *Hot Chocolates*, a musical revue written by composer Fats Waller. Louis sang Waller's "Ain't Misbehavin'" so well from the orchestra pit that audiences insisted he sing it onstage.

To this point in his career, Louis had performed only at nightclubs. Now his great talent was on display on one of the biggest stages in the country. *Hot Chocolates* opened in 1929. Critics raved about Louis's performance. As the Roaring Twenties came to an end, Louis Armstrong was positioned to become a major star.

END OF THE JAZZ AGE

It can sometimes be difficult to tell when one historical era ends and another begins. But the end of the Jazz Age was sparked by a very particular event.

On October 29, 1929, the stock market crashed. After a decade of high living, many Americans lost all the money they had overnight. The country was plunged into the worst **economic** crisis in history.

About thirteen million Americans were out of work. The country looked to President Herbert Hoover for relief. However, Hoover felt it was best to let the situation turn around on its own. Meanwhile, unemployed and homeless Americans lived in city parks that were called Hoovervilles.

The next president, Franklin Roosevelt, signed many laws aimed at providing jobs and relief to the nation's poor. Still, the Great Depression lasted through the 1930s. It was one of most difficult periods in American history.

Newspaper headlines announce the stock market crash, the start of a widespread panic that swept the nation in October of 1929.

* * * *

Many people were forced to beg for work during the Great Depression.

END OF PROHIBITION

In 1932, Congress agreed that the experiment with Prohibition had failed. On December 5, 1933, the Twenty-first Amendment made the drinking of alcohol legal once more. The speakeasies of the Jazz Age closed, and **bootleggers** went out of business.

In such hard times, the attitude of the country changed instantly. The party of the 1920s was over, replaced by a period of hardship. Though Americans continued to listen to jazz, the high spirits that defined the Jazz Age were gone.

As part of his tour in Europe, Louis Armstrong performed at Olympia Music Hall in Paris, France, in December 1955.

At the end of the 1920s, Louis Armstrong was still a young man with a good forty years of music making ahead of him. He was admired by generation after generation of musicians and music lovers. He traveled the world with a number of all-star bands. After a successful tour of Europe in 1955, the *New York Times* wrote, "America's secret weapon is a blue note in a minor key. Right now its most successful ambassador is Louis Satchmo Armstrong."

Of course Louis had some critics. In the late 1940s a new kind of jazz called bebop became popular among black musicians. Louis's type of music was called old-fashioned. But to the end, Louis loved playing the hot New Orleans jazz that he made famous.

When Louis died on July 6, 1971, people across the world felt a great sense of loss. He was more than just one of the country's most beloved entertainers. Louis was the driving force behind the creation of America's most distinctive art form, jazz.

By the time he died, Louis was famous around the world. According to South African trumpet player Hugh Masekela, "Louis Armstrong loosened the world, helped people to be able to say 'Yeah,' and to walk with a little dip in their hip. Before Louis Armstrong, the world was definitely square, just like Christopher Columbus thought."

This photograph shows Louis and his wife, Lucille, in 1971.

HAPPILY MARRIED AT LAST

When Louis moved to New York in 1929, he and Lil grew apart. They divorced in 1931. After a brief marriage to a dancer, Louis finally settled down with his fourth wife, Lucille Wilson. They married in 1942. Louis and Lucille lived for the rest of their lives in a small house they bought in Queens, New York. Today it is a museum.

41

Glossary

accompany—in music, to support or complement a melody either by singing or playing an instrument

beverage—drink

bootleggers—people who make or sell illegal liquor

brass band—a group of musicians playing only brass instruments (such as the trumpet or the trombone) or percussion instruments (such as cymbals or a bass drum)

conductor—person who leads a musical group

cornet—brass musical instrument that looks like a shortened trumpet

discrimination—treating someone differently based on the person's race, religion, or other traits

economic—relating to money

improvisation—the act of making something up on
the spot

Judaism—the Jewish religion

mute—in jazz, a device placed in the mouth of a brass
instrument to soften the sound

native—born of a certain place or country

prohibiting—stopping or forbidding

technique—skill or craftsmanship

trousers—pants

wayward—disobedient

Timeline: Louis Armstrong

1901	1912	1914	1918	1919	1920	1922
Louis Armstrong is born in New Orleans.	Louis is arrested and sent to the Waif's Home, where he learns to play the trumpet.	Louis is released from the Waif's Home and becomes recognized as one of the best trumpet players in New Orleans.	Louis replaces Joe Oliver in Kid Ory's band.	World War I ends.	Prohibition outlawing alcohol begins.	Louis moves to Chicago to join Joe Oliver's Creole Jazz Band.

and the Jazz Age

1924	1925	1926	1928	1929

1924

Louis moves to New York to play with Fletcher Henderson's Black Swan Troubadours.

1925

Louis makes the first Hot Five recordings.

1926

Scat song "Heebie Jeebies" becomes a hit.

1928

Louis records *West End Blues*, thought by many to be the best jazz record ever made.

1929

Louis appears in *Hot Chocolates* on Broadway. The stock market crashes, hurtling America into the Great Depression. The Jazz Age ends.

To Find Out More

BOOKS

Collier, James Lincoln. *The Louis Armstrong You Never Knew*. Danbury, CT: Children's Press, 2004.

Feinstein, Stephen. *The 1920s from Prohibition to Charles Lindbergh*. Berkeley Heights, NJ: Enslow, 2001.

Jordan, Denise. *Harlem Renaissance Artists*. Chicago: Heinemann Library, 2003.

ONLINE SITES

Jazz at Lincoln Center
http://www.jazzatlincolncenter.org/educ/curriculum/modules/ LouisArmstrong/module.html

PBS Jazz Kids
http://www.pbs.org/jazz/kids/

Smithsonian Jazz Class
http://www.smithsonianjazz.org/class/armstrong/la_match.asp

Index

Bold numbers indicate illustrations.

About the Author

Dan Elish is the author of numerous books for children, including *The Worldwide Dessert Contest* and *Born Too Short, the Confessions of an Eighth-Grade Basket Case*, which was picked as a 2003 Book for the Teen Age by the New York Public Library. He lives in New York City with his wife and daughter.